Our World

James Reyes-Picknell

Published by James Reyes-Picknell, 2024.

OUR WORLD

First edition. June 14, 2024.

Copyright © 2024 James Reyes-Picknell.

ISBN: 979-8227158727

Written by James Reyes-Picknell.

Table of Contents

This book is dedicated to those who work in industries and in jobs we rarely think about, as well as the children, now in school, who someday will take their places.

OUR WORLD:
ONE BIG ECOSYSTEM

GRADES 7, 8, 9

By: James Reyes-Picknell

FOREWORD

I didn't know the author of "Our World", James, until he approached me to ask if my name could be included in the book's acknowledgements. He had attended a mining discussion forum where I expressed my concerns about the general lack of knowledge in young people, about industries like mining, and how our education system just seems to miss the mark. Young potential employees have impressions that are often incorrect. Consequently, they don't consider careers in these essential industries. I suggested that we need to do a better job educating our youth about the good we do in industry, and show them that there are careers out there, that they could be missing.

That was all it took. Apparently, it inspired James enough to write, "Our World". I read the draft copy and in two words, "love it!!!"

James consults to industrial companies and he is already a well-known published author and speaker in his field. "Our World" is aimed at a much younger and arguably more important audience - our children and grand-children. The time is right, I believe "Our World" hits the mark and is something that children, their parents, teachers and guidance counsellors should be exposed to.

It can only help!

Mark Cutifani, Chairman, Vale Base Metals

PREFACE

It is my sincere desire that this book makes your curious. Curious about the world around you, about how things work, and about the opportunities it offers to you.

I work as a management consultant and do a lot of work in mining. It's an industry that many don't know much about. I see some good things happening in mines and in the communities where they are located. But the industry has difficulty attracting new talent to fill some very good jobs. Those jobs pay very well, but mining companies still have trouble, and I wondered why. Industry image turns out to be a big part of the problem.

Mining has had a bad image that is only slowly improving. It is not often seen as a cool place to work. To many it appears to be a dirty and polluting industry. That image often goes against the values of those younger people it is trying to hire. Mines are often in remote locations where most younger people want to live. Not much can be done about locations – those are determined by nature's placement of minerals in our earth. But life in those communities can also be very nice. The image problem is because most people don't know much about the industry, and what they do know is not entirely accurate.

Most other heavy industries like oil and gas, pulp and paper, and chemicals, are also struggle with the problems. But the industry can only do so much, the image can only change gradually over time. It is a problem in the minds of people who are uninformed.

That bad image is largely a result of past bad behavior. But today, most have cleaned up their act a lot. There's still old damage to be undone, but the first step is to stop doing harm. The industry has taken that step.

To go further with the cleanup, the industry needs new talent, and new ideas – your ideas.

However, so long as old image is a "turn off" for younger potential employees it will starve them of the talent they need.

At a mining conference, one mining company president did a great job of describing the good that his company, and others, are doing. He also expressed frustration that far too few outside the industry are even aware of it. Lack of awareness comes from a lack of exposure. Most people get exposed to new ideas while they are in school, so why not start there. He suggested, and I agree, that the education system has a role to play. This book is an attempt to help dispel that image. If the book is read by children in school, it can help to make a difference that we can all benefit from.

Teachers, guidance counsellors and parents all need to learn about the opportunities that exist for their children and students. Our education system doesn't always produce people who are equipped to work in many of the jobs that need to be done. That is in part because people don't know what is needed in the job market and school boards do little to address that knowledge gap. And that is because many educational administrators, school board trustees, teachers and guidance counsellors don't really know much about other industries and the opportunities that exist.

Most don't know much about mining and the good it is actually doing in many communities. They don't realize that without mines the electric car that everyone wants to be driving to work wouldn't exist.

Without knowledge, how can one teach others?

This book was inspired by that need. It is written largely for children and intended to be tool for the school boards, teachers, guidance counselors, and even parents, who can use it to teach those children.

My intention is to generate curiosity. To show how our industries are interconnected and how important they are to our society and to encourage children to ask about everything they see around them. We simply cannot live as we do without some of those industries. We should understand and appreciate that many aspects of our lives, like cell phones, eco-friendly electric cars, and low-energy housing are dependent on industries that we often look down upon.

I also want to show that those industries offer some terrific opportunities as career choices.

This book is about shattering some old images with an honest portrayal of what those industries are like today and opening young peoples' eyes to opportunities they may otherwise miss. Be curious, ask questions and find the answers.

ACKNOWLEDGEMENTS

This is for all those who inspired and helped me in creating this – my first non-technical book.

Inspiration for the idea came from comments by Mark Cutifani, Chairman of Base Metals for the mining company, Vale SA, here in Canada. He spoke at a panel session organized by the consulting firm, EY Canada. Mark was lamenting the image problem within the mining industry and the fact that so few, except those who lived near mines, really seemed to understand the truth about the good they actually do. He challenged the audience to find ways of getting past that image. Later discussions led to the idea of educating younger people, while still in school, about the realities and not just the image.

Several helped with encouragement, moral support and by reviewing drafts of the book. My wife, Aileen, who takes care of my needs and is always encouraging me to try something new. For me, a book that is intended for children is indeed new. Without that encouragement, transforming Mark's ideas into a real book may not have happened.

Several reviewers helped with their reactions to the book concept and content. Their ideas, feedback and encouragement are all deeply appreciated.

Among those reviewers are my wife, Aileen, my youngest sister, Monica Fusco, neighbors the Rolph family, Evelyn Robinson, and a colleague, Brenda Roberts, Human Resources Manager at New Gold Inc's Rainy River operations. All of your inputs were taken to heart and led to many revisions and corrections in that first draft.

As a result of your comments and suggestions, wording was changed, factual errors checked and corrected, examples simplified and some was translated into Tween! Thank you all!

Thanks also for your candid thoughts about my early attempts at artwork. Perhaps I'm too far along for lessons in art, and I've realized that I really should stick to writing! With your encouragement I sought and found help! Aileen, thanks for your help in finding Monika Yee. Monika is daughter of a good friend, who just happens to be a skilled artist about to embark on her college education. Her creativity led to production of the artwork for both the cover and throughout the book. Thank you, Monika.

Finally, a big "thank you" (in advance) to all the adults who will see fit to share this with the children in your lives.

INTRODUCTION FOR ADULTS

This book will explain the connections from everyday objects, that many of us take for granted, back to the sources of their materials and how they were made. Each connection employs people in a variety of jobs or roles that may not be visible or well-known, yet they are vital. Even those engaged in managing the companies that perform these various tasks are often not well known, but they are no less vital in supporting our way of life.

Baby boomers are mostly retired and Gen X is beginning to retire. With older people retiring and many younger ones starting, the workforce today is actually getting younger.

Those working include Gen Y (millennials – who were born between the late 70's and mid-90's), Gen Z (iGen or Centennials – who were born between the mid-90s and about 2015), and Gen A (alpha – born since 2015).

Generations Y and Z are either in, or entering the workforce right now. Along with Gen A, they tend to be very comfortable with technology and they know how to use it. Gen Z are the first ever "digital natives" who have grown up entirely within the internet age.

Many of those want jobs in the tech industries. Tech companies have done a great job expressing social values that match those of younger generations. The downside of that has been that many younger workers have less desire to work in traditional industries. Those industries are not high tech, and may even have work environments requiring more "hands on". They are seen by some as dirty, too far from home, and possibly even too remote.

Those traditional industries use tech, but produce materials and products that we all use, even if we don't realize it. Materials like steel in our cars and buildings, paper, fossil fuels, the materials is our phones, the gold in our jewelry and so much more.

Companies in these traditional industries often struggle to find workers with the right skills to match their needs. The jobs they offer, can be very high paying, yet remain vacant for a long time. Those vacant jobs are often in fields that require hands-on work – high touch, not high tech. They are jobs like mechanics, millwrights, electricians, welders, instrumentation technicians, fitters, communications, electronics, and robotics technicians. Those skills are learned after high school. The require a combination of post-secondary education in college with practical application in an apprenticeship.

Those jobs are perceived as "dirty" or "blue collar", despite the education needed to do them.

Historically "blue collar" did mean they required less education and more brawn. But today that's simply not the case. They require more education and skill than ever. Yet fewer young people choose those career paths because they don't know much about them. They may be put off by the old "image" industrial employers and attracted to industries that are better at marketing – like computers and tech.

While tech appears to be more attractive, it doesn't always pay as well as some expect. The "high pay" image was once true, but that has changed. The old image was formed when computerization was growing rapidly, there were many high-tech opportunities, and not so many applicants. Now we have more tech workers, a growing supply, and less demand. The best job opportunities may well be elsewhere but less well known.

Location matters to job seekers. Most prefer to work where they are familiar, close to home, or where they expect "excitement" – often in a bigger urban center. Bigger cities are more attractive, but they have much more competition for jobs, and sometimes a higher cost of living.

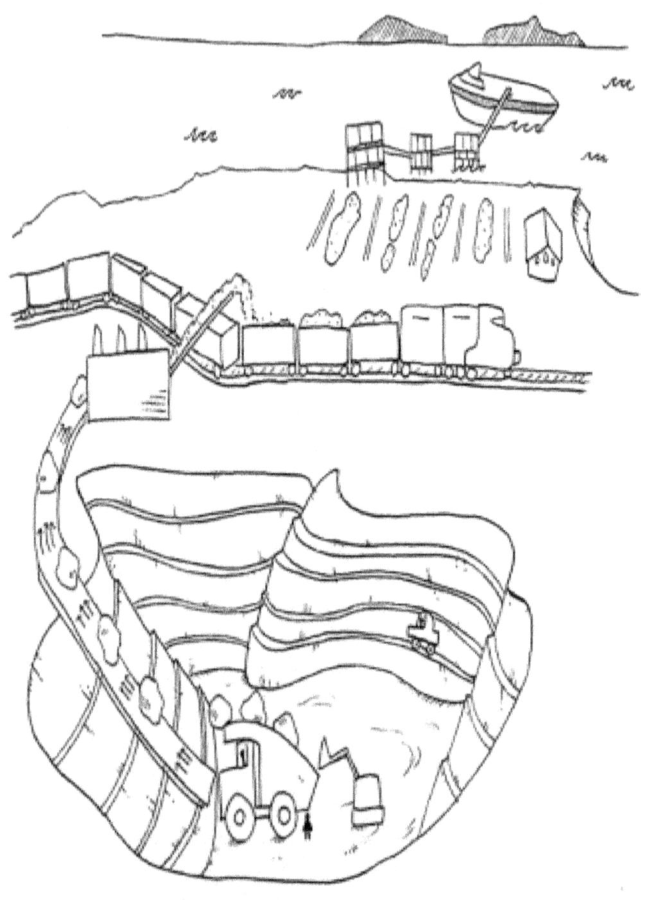

1 Mine, ore processing, then shipping by rail and ship to anywhere in the world

LET'S LOOK AT MINING. The industry has had a bad image and hasn't yet done much to change it. Those in the industry know that the reality is far better though. Mining supports the livelihoods of thousands of workers and their families. Many whole communities are employed and supported by the industry. As an industry, it is working hard to maintain safe work places, to reduce emissions, achieve greater gender equality, diversity, and provide for a healthy work-life balance.

The state of planet and the people who populate it are at an important inflection point, both in terms of human and earth history. Humanity is faced with a crisis of pollution, environmental harm, and global climate change. Those are all influenced by human activity. A lot of the problem comes from past practices that have now changed, at least in many developed nations. Today most industries work hard to clean up their act, and then to clean up their mess, even if they were created long ago. To do that, they need new thinking, ideas and innovation. They need younger well-educated workers, enthusiasm, passion and their ideas.

To fix it, we also need to understand how it is working now so we can find the flaws. We also need to look inward – into ourselves and our own behaviors. We could all benefit from a shift to a less selfish concern about the common good.

Some activists want to shut down "dirty" industries. That would be nice, it is also an unrealistic and overly simplistic solution. Without viable alternatives we only shift the problem elsewhere.

For example, if we move to all-electric transportation to reduce our use of fossil fuels, we will need a lot more renewable electric power generation, and far more copper than the world can produce today. But if we get rid of mines, how will we do it?

We have already replaced a lot of paper with electronics (e.g.: newspapers with i-pads (tablets) and laptops). It helps reduce the use of trees, but increases use of oil (in plastics), and various mining products to make all of that electronic hardware. Trees can regrow, and they capture carbon as they do so. Minerals do not.

This book doesn't provide all the answers to those weighty questions and issues, but it is intended to get us thinking and to enable the reader to begin making choices that will help them become a part of the solutions we need to find.

Our school systems have not always provided the education that our youth need to make informed choices about their own future. Our children learn some of the basics, some develop a higher sense of purpose than older generations, and some may even have many ideas on how to fix our broken world and societies. There is an urgency to act quickly that fits their temperament, but they need help seeing how they can help.

They need a better grounding in basics, science and common sense to help them make better choices.

Industries have messed things up in response to consumer demand. By wanting it all, wanting convenience, and wanting it cheap, we have asked for that. We know better but we don't always act better.

To help those industries clean-up we need people in jobs that might not seem so "cool". By explaining more about them, perhaps they'll become more attractive.

OUR WORLD

Many are unaware of all the options available because we haven't been taught about them. This book should help with that at least a little bit.

Here in this book, it all starts by looking at everyday objects like cell phones, houses, books or kitchen appliances. Each is a product of a complex combination of materials and manufacturing methods, each with its own chain of suppliers, and workers. Many of those workers' jobs are very interesting too!

By asking questions about the objects in our hands we can begin to see the many options that are out there. We may find some to be interesting. We may find some that are not. We can begin to see the need for education and skills development that we will need if we want a career in those areas. We can start earlier with our choices. Doing this keeps more options open. It's never a good idea to wait until school ends to find out that our past choices have limited our options!

The book is organized to follow "a day in the life" of a young person, from awakening to going back to sleep. A few chapters speak to the unseen aspects of keeping everything running smoothly, at home, in businesses, and in government. It is my hope that by describing all the varied aspects of life as the reader encounters it, she or he will gain some additional knowledge and above all, curiosity.

INTRODUCTION FOR STUDENTS

Ask questions and then go find the answers. That's how can all learn a great deal. You can ask about where things around you come from. How are they made? Who makes them? What sort of jobs do people have to make them?

This book asks a lot of questions. It answers some of them. It is meant to demonstrate how, by asking questions, we can learn a lot. The world around us is filled with the products of many industries and many people who work in those industries. Some of those jobs might be of great interest to you, if you know it is there and you know a little about it.

In my work we do a lot of problem solving for big companies The simplest and most effective way to do that is to keep asking "why", "what", "when" and "who"? Why did that happen? What happened before that? Why did that happen? And Who was it that made that mistake? Why did they make that mistake? And so on...

In this book we'll go through a day in your life and ask a lot of questions. How many of the questions that we asked, did you know the answer to, before you read it here? If the answer is, "a lot", then you have a very curious mind – you like to explore. If you answered, "not many", then you can cultivate that curiosity.

Why would you want to do that? Because it makes you more aware of opportunities that are there for you. One day you will want to find work. You'll want it to pay well and support your life style. You may want it to pay enough to support your own family. You may want it to be in a community that is clean, that has access to wilderness locations, or to big city fun. The choices you make about school and later about your career, will make those things you want available to you. If you make a choice that doesn't give you what you want, then you can keep asking questions and find an alternative choice that does.

To get your curiosity going let's dive right in.

A DAY IN YOUR LIFE

Each day we are in contact with and use a variety of things and services. Many are taken for granted and only really noticed if they go "off". If you flip a switch and the lights don't go on you begin to wonder what's wrong. You try it again – the same result. You try another light, perhaps in another room and see if it works. If it doesn't you might look outside to see if streetlights are on, or if houses across the street have any lights on. You look to see if you have a cell phone signal and if there is any news about a power outage. All that was triggered by a light that didn't come on. If the lights come on soon, that curiosity dies away quickly and you get on with your normal day.

We take a lot of what is around us for granted. Many of us remain blissfully unaware of what it takes to get power to that light, to put those walls around your room, to produce the clothes you put on, to get your breakfast meal to the table or to get you to school.

Let's look at what you do from the time you get up to the time you go to bed again.

An alarm probably wakes you up – it might be on your phone if you have one, or it might be a clock with an alarm in your bedroom. Failing that, your parents probably get you up, perhaps after a few attempts. But what got them up?

OUR WORLD

You might have showered before bed, or you might shower when you wake up so you can start the day fresh. How did the water get there? How did it get hot?

You dry yourself off and get dressed. Where did those clothes come from? Are they natural fibers or synthetic? How did they get colored and sized? What is involved in making sure they are fresh and clean?

Once dressed, you head to the kitchen for some breakfast. One of your parents is probably getting breakfast ready for you. Whether it is cereal in a bowl, bacon and eggs, or some other favorite, you eat. Where did the food come from? Aside from mom or dad putting it there, how did it get to your kitchen so they could put it on your table?

After eating you brush your teeth, grab your school bag and maybe a lunch. Where did the toothpaste come from? How did that school bag get made? What about the books, pens, pencils, and other items inside it? How is your lunch packed for you? Is it in waxed paper wrappers or plastic containers? How does the thermos keep the soup warm?

You walk to the school bus stop or hop in your parent's car for the ride to school. How was that bus or car built? Where did the materials that make up the tires, the body, the seating, and the lights all come from? How was it built? Where was it built? Who organized the route it follows to get you to school on time for classes?

Inside the school, you have a locker. You unlock and open it, hang your jacket and put your lunch inside, grab the books you need for your classes and lock it back up. What makes up that lock? What is the locker made of? Where did its parts come from – the lock, the hinges, the door?

You can hang up your jacket in winter because the building is comfortably warm inside. In summer it is kept cool with air conditioning. How do those work? How does it happen that you get the right amount of heating in winter and cooling in summer? If they break, who fixes it?

In class and at home you are working with books, and perhaps your i-pad. Your teacher presents on a screen, or using felt pens on a whiteboard. Where did all of those come from? The teacher knows more about the subjects than you do. How did the teacher learn all that?

You move from class to class, subject to subject, at preset times. The bell rings indicating breaks and lunch. The classrooms are full of desks, white boards, video equipment. The walls, doors, windows are all the same from room to room. How were they made, and who decided on class room design? Classes take place at the same times every day. Who determines the schedule? Who determines what will be taught and how it will be taught? Who teaches the teachers?

At lunch, you go to a cafeteria where you can eat the lunch your parents prepared, add juice or milk to it, or even buy your whole lunch there. How did the milk, juice, and food get to the cafeteria? Who prepares and serves it?

After school, you might play sports or head home. You might get on a computer gaming console. Where did that come from? How is it that you can game with people in other locations? It's fun and it works quickly. You need good reflexes and a quick eye. How does it work so fast, even when the person you are playing with is a long way from you, maybe even in another city?

Finally, it's off the bed.

OUR WORLD

Some days, perhaps on weekends, you might go to the mall, shopping, or tag along with friends to simply "hang out". There are a lot of stores each stocked full of products. How do those products get there? What are they made of? Where does that raw material come from? Who designs the clothing and shoes? Who sews the clothing? Who makes the shoes?

How did the mall get there? Who was involved? How much work is it to build it? How did they know a mall was needed? And how did they know that was the best place for it?

All the time, you are getting around on roads and highways. How do they end up where they are? What are they made of? Where does that come from?

You probably see police, paramedics, ambulances, fire trucks, municipal vehicles for road repair, snow clearing and other jobs that the city looks after. Where do they come from? Why do we need them? Why does the city look after them and not someone else?

These are all questions about the things and services we experience in our everyday lives. The following chapters will delve into those questions. You will begin to see that like an iceberg, what you see and experience first, isn't the whole picture. There is usually much more happening behind the scenes.

TURNING ON THE LIGHTS

When it's dark we turn on the lights by flipping a switch. That allows electricity to flow to the light. It lights up and it gets warm. The light is what you want, the warmth is a by-product. That light, like so many of our inventions, is not 100% efficient. The extra energy going into heat is effectively wasted unless you can capture it and use it for something that needs heat.

A big problem in our world today is that we get too much of our energy from sources that can't be replaced easily or at a reasonable cost. Those are "non-renewable" sources – like burning oil to run a power generator. If the power comes from a wind turbine or a hydroelectric generating station, it is "renewable" because there is always going to be wind and water flowing from high to low elevations.

Non-renewable sources do get used up, and they create pollution which harms our environment. The environment is what we depend on for those renewable resources like wind and water.

Let's look at how the electricity gets to the light bulb.

The light switch, the conductive wires that bring the electricity to the light, and the systems bringing electricity to your house are all connected.

Some materials (like plastic and ceramics) insulate rather than conduct electricity. We use those to protect us. The conductor itself is a material, usually a metal like copper.

Different materials conduct better than others. The best won't waste as much of the energy by heating up. Copper is also flexible making it easy to install in your house.

2 Electrical distribution to your house

OUTSIDE YOUR HOME, the wires are either buried underground or strung up on poles. That keeps people and animals from touching them and being hurt. If they touch the wires, they could be shocked and killed by the electricity. The wires are mounted on, and surrounded by insulators like the plastic coating over the wire. It prevents you (and anything else around it) from touching the parts of the wire that have the electricity flowing. In your neighborhood the wiring is managed by your electric distribution company and the electricians who work there.

Those wires are connected together with all the other houses in your neighborhood, and the neighborhoods in your city in what is called an electrical distribution network. Networks like that are designed by electrical engineers to make sure that all the houses get enough electricity. The electricity is generated and usually far away.

Most cities don't have their own power generation. The electricity must be conducted from where it is generated to the distribution network. If the power plant is far away, the electricity is transmitted in larger wires from the power plant to the distribution network. That long-distance transfer of the electricity is known as "transmission". The power plant itself must create electricity by converting some other form of energy such as fuel, water pressure, nuclear energy, wind, solar, and tidal effects. Some of those are renewable and considered "clean" sources of energy (wind, solar, tidal), some are dirty (hydrocarbon-fired plants), and one is clean, long-lasting, but not renewable – nuclear. Nuclear also produces hazardous waste that must be managed, but it doesn't pollute like hydrocarbons.

Those generation plants contain equipment that converts the energy from its source into electricity through a generator. The plant equipment itself is made of materials like iron, steel, and copper.

Electric generation, transmission and distribution creates a lot of work for electricians, electrical engineers, power plant operators, technicians, and all the administrative staff to make sure you pay for what you use. All of them require a higher education in college or university to get those jobs.

Copper, the material in wires, comes from copper mines. We don't find electrical wires in nature. We have to make them. We rarely find copper in big chunks of pure copper. It is usually mixed in with other minerals and a lot of rock that we don't have use for. We need to find the copper in the earth, and then extract it from all that rock and separate it from the other minerals. The chemical processes for doing that extraction are designed by chemical engineers. Finding the copper in the earth is done by geologists.

A mine is where we get our minerals. We can extract copper (and other minerals) for use in all sorts of applications. The earth is made up of many minerals. In some places, those minerals are concentrated more than others. In those areas where there are high enough concentrations of minerals, we can build a mine to extract the minerals we want at a reasonable cost. Mining involves digging up the earth in those areas, getting rid of any non-mineral bearing earth that might be in the way, and then processing the earth that has the minerals to extract them.

Sometimes the minerals we want are deep underground so we dig deep tunnels to get to them so we can process them and extract the minerals so we get concentrations that we can actually use. When using tunnelling we are doing "underground" mining. In some areas the minerals are near the surface of the earth, so instead of tunnelling to get to them, we dig big holes or pits. When we dig the big pits, we are doing surface mining, or "open pit" mining. Both types of mining are disruptive to the earth where the minerals are found. Mines are complicated and they can be dangerous, especially under-ground. A lot of care goes into designing them to be safe – something that mine engineers take care of.

Usually, minerals are found in fairly low concentrations. The earth we remove and process contains only a small fraction of what we want. Earth that doesn't contain what we want, but must be removed first, is called "over-burden" or "waste-rock", and it is moved out of the way. At mines, you often see large piles of earth that have been put there. That is usually an overburden. Overburden, and the waste from the chemical processing (known as tailings), are what make mines look unpleasant. There are large quantities of both that must be managed to ensure we don't harm the environment or ecology in the area of a mine.

The earth and rock that contains the minerals we want will be processed in an ore processing plant. It contains tanks, crushers, mills, chemical processing vessels, filters, driers, conveyors and other equipment used in extracting the minerals from the rock. Large pieces of rock from the mine are crushed into smaller pieces and then put into a mill where they are broken down even further into very small particles which are then chemically treated to extract the minerals. The chemical solutions with the minerals are then processed chemically and in filters to separate the minerals from the chemicals to produce a concentrate. That's then dried and stored, eventually shipped off for further refinement (chemically) or to be used as it is. Design of those processing plants requires a good deal of chemical, mechanical and electrical engineering. Building them requires mechanics, electricians, instrumentation technicians, steel workers, welders, construction crews, truckers, and more.

The mining and extraction processes use a lot of energy. The mine itself uses a lot of fuel to power drills, shovels and trucks to break the earth up into manageable pieces and move them to the crushers and processing plants. Most of that energy is stored in the form of fuel (in tanks), or in batteries that must be charged. Many mines are a long way from bigger cities and electric power transmission systems, so they actually have their own power generation stations.

The trucks, drills, shovels, loaders, and processing equipment are all made of materials like iron, copper, steel, rubber and other materials. Many of those materials are also mined. Some, like rubber, are produced from chemicals and oil. Oil extraction is similar to mining. We find concentrations of oil underground or near the surface and process it into fuels and other useful products.

Plastics, many forms of rubber, and even materials used in making clothing (polyester, nylon) are actually products made by processing oil from the ground. Those chemicals are formed into fibers, threads and woven into textile sheets.

It can be said that if we don't grow it (like plants and animals), then we must mine it. Many of the products we use every day are made from materials that must be mined. Although mining is very disruptive to the land, the ecology and the area of the mine itself, it is still needed if we are to sustain our convenient life style. Today, mines and their processes are designed to minimize their negative impacts so that the businesses that run them can be profitable while ensuring the environment is sustained as best they can. In many mines, the land is actually returned to a natural state, albeit without the minerals that were being mined. The mining industry actually employs many environmental engineers and technicians and makes extensive use of laboratories to make sure that it is keeping the environment clean.

Copper is just one example. We also mine for iron, nickel and other minerals used to make steel and stainless steel. We mine for gold, silver, diamonds, other gemstones, coal (a fuel), lead, cobalt, uranium (nuclear fuel), etc.

Without the mines that produce those basic materials, we wouldn't have most of the products we use every day and take for granted. We wouldn't be able to generate electricity and move it from where it is generated to where we use it through those transmission and distribution networks. We wouldn't have the pipes underground that supply our house with water and carry away our waste. We wouldn't have garbage trucks to collect trash and recyclables. Of course, we also wouldn't have anything to recycle – we'd basically live our lives in tents, eating only what we can grow or catch locally with our hands, much like cave-people.

Primitive life was hard, so even the cave-people learned to use tools. At first, they were made of stone which was easily found and could be shaped to make the hunting job easier. The skins of the animals killed for food were used for clothing to keep them warm. Fire was used to cook food and make it easier to digest. The fire was fueled by wood and eventually coal was discovered. Some oils from animals were also discovered to be flammable and used to fuel fires used to heat and cook. As history progressed, we found useful minerals like copper, learned how to extract them and made tools and weapons from it. Mixing it with other minerals, like tin, resulted in bronze, a material with even more utility. Copper and bronze are fairly soft and don't last long when used a lot. Iron was found to be more difficult to extract and work into tools and weapons, but it was also much stronger. Mixing it with carbon (from coal fires) resulted in steel – even stronger and more flexible. Mixing with a small amount of nickel made it less prone to rusting. That's stainless steel.

As history progressed humanity's knowledge of materials and what they can do has grown. That knowledge enabled more human growth and more human growth enabled more discovery and innovation.

Finding minerals requires a great deal of exploratory effort on the part of geologists. Getting those minerals from where they are found to where we can use them, requires extensive transportation networks. Fueling the transport requires an energy industry. The roads, railroads, and waterways we use for transport require engineering and maintenance.

You can imagine, that much of what we have around us is provided from a variety of diverse sources, and that it took a lot of effort to provide it. Each part of that effort represents opportunities for economic activity and many very interesting jobs.

TAKING A SHOWER

Not long after you get up, or before you go to bed, you probably take a bath or a shower. You use soap and shampoo with warm water to clean dirt and grime off your body and hair. The soap and shampoo are manufactured for us using a combination of chemicals, oils and animal fats. Those have unique properties of being able to cut through grease or oils, creating a cleansing foam that helps loosen dirt so that the water can rinse it away, and leaving us with a nice smelling residue that is not harmful to our skin or health. We feel fresh.

The soap had to be designed by chemists, and then manufactured in a factory somewhere and transported from that factory to the store where it was bought, and then to your home for you to use it. The factory that produced it uses raw materials such as oil, water, lye and other chemicals. It combines them in chemical reactors to produce the product you use. It is put into bottles, or shaped and wrapped for delivery to stores. Those factories may also produce other products, often soaps for doing dishes, use in dishwashers and for laundry.

The soap alone required chemical engineers, chemists, farmers for some of the raw materials, mining, oil extractions, and the building of factories by engineers and construction workers. The manufacture of soap is a chemical process aided by mechanical equipment. The manufacture of bottles and packaging materials for it require different sorts of factories and processes. All of those require a great deal of thought and organization on the part of the engineers and technicians who make them.

Some soaps and shampoos are more complicated to make than others. The fragrance, the softeners that are added, the hardener to make bars, and the liquid base for use in handpumps all add complexity to the manufacturing process.

The water had to be transported to your home and kept pressurized so it could be used in your shower and heated. Without the pressure, your shower will be a drip at best. The water was carried in pipes made of copper, iron, or various plastics.

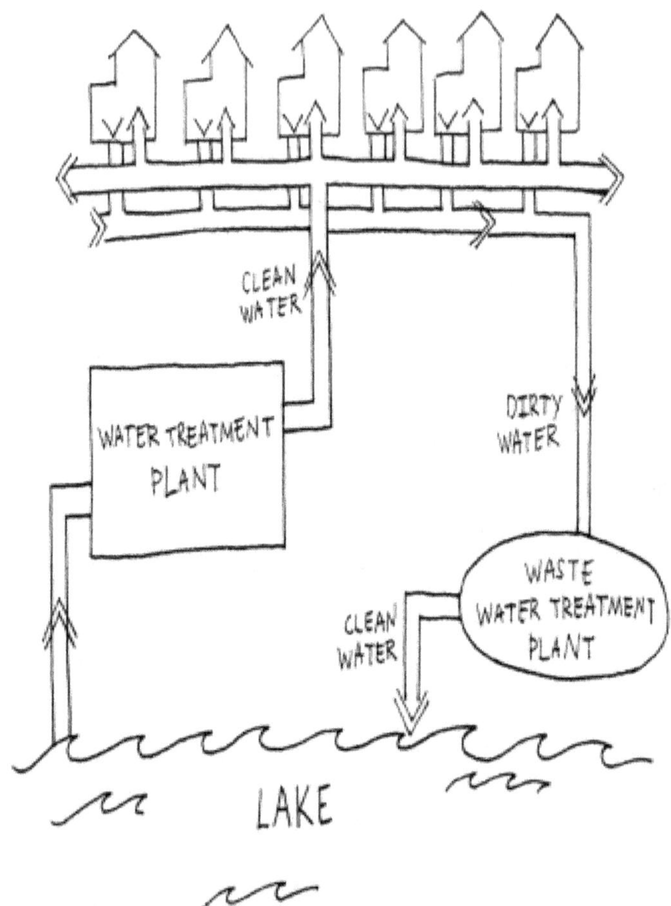

3 Water and waste water for your home

WATER, GAS AND ELECTRICITY

Water for your home may come from a well on your property, or via a series of pipes in your city from a water treatment plant. The treatment plant cleans the water using filters and ultraviolet light to remove particulates and contaminants that are found in the water source. Chemical analysis is used to make sure it is pure enough for drinking and safe for use. The water may be from a lake, a river, or wells. Often it isn't quite as clear as you see in your home – that clarity and freedom from contaminants is achieved in the water treatment plant. Running those plants requires engineers, trades persons, chemists, and administrative staff. Building the water networks requires a great deal of excavation of the ground, installation of pipes and a design that ensures the water that reaches your house has sufficient pressure and volume to be useful.

After treating the water, it is then piped into a network by large pumps and kept pressurized by those pumps and tall water towers. Those towers with multiple legs, have tanks at the top containing the water for your home. The height is what maintains the pressure.

The water gets there through pipes. The tank and the legs holding it up are made of steel and painted to prevent corrosion. Often, the tanks have the name of your city painted on them too!

That water in your shower is also warm, so it is heated for your use, in a water heater that is heated by fuel (a non-renewable hydro-carbon like natural gas) or electricity. Your future choice of hot water heater can actually impact our environment!

Hot water from the heater is mixed with cooler water to the temperature that you find comfortable by a mixing valve right there in the shower. It's a fairly complicated valve manufactured from materials that, like the piping, were all mined. It has rubber parts inside to keep the hot and cold water separated until mixed when you turn the shower on. It is also designed to maintain a constant temperature that you set by adjusting it. That is done using moving parts and an expandable type of wax. Some clever design work went into it.

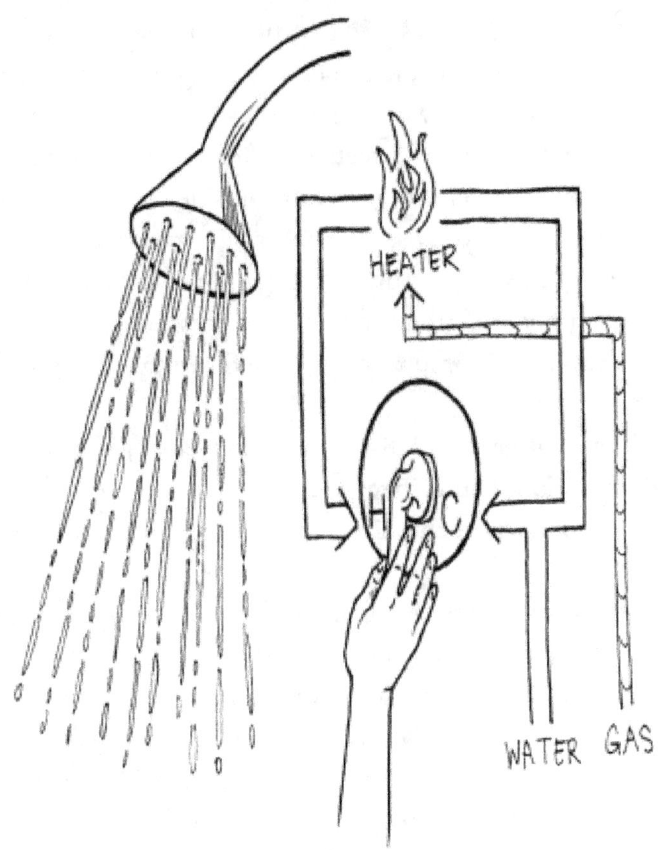

4 Heating water for your shower

THE WATER HEATER MAY be heated by electricity or gas fuel that is piped to your home. Gas, like water, is piped to where it is used. There is an extensive network of pipes for both water and gas under the streets and sidewalks of your home. They both have meters (in or on the outside of your home) to measure how much you use. The water pipes come from a water treatment plant and pressure is maintained by towers. The gas comes from a gas distribution plant and pressure is maintained by compressors. A compressor is a machine that adds pressure to a gas.

Water treatment and distribution, as well as gas processing and distribution require extensive networks and a lot of skilled workers. Engineers, technicians, trades and laborers are needed by both.

The gas distribution plant adds a small amount of a chemical that smells bad (mercaptan) for safety. Since the gas is colorless and odorless, but highly flammable, we don't want it to leak without some way of knowing that it is leaking. The mercaptan makes sure we can smell it and since it's a bad smell, we are more likely to want to fix the leak quickly.

The mercaptan is a chemical produced in a chemical plant. The gas occurs naturally and is usually found with oil, deep underground. Oil and gas are both extracted from the earth using wells and various extraction technologies. When they come to the surface, they are mixed and often contain water and other chemicals that can be harmful. At the surface, there are processing plants that separate the oil gas and water, extract the harmful chemicals, and store the finished products for shipment via trucks or pipelines. The oil from the ground needs to be processed in a refinery into products like gasoline, aircraft fuel, heating fuel, waxes, and even tar which can be used in paving roads. Gas usually needs very little processes except separation from water, oil and other chemicals, before it is ready to be piped away to be used.

You'll find engineers, trades, technicians, chemists, laborers and others all working oil and gas fields, in the processing plants and on the piping systems that get the products (oil, gas, chemicals) to manufacturing plants and your home.

OIL AND GAS

Oil and gas are found in nature, deep underground, either on land or underwater. Where they are found, you can find oil and gas extraction machinery like piping, pumps, compressors and separation plants. Those areas are known as oil and gas fields. Some are on land like Alberta in western Canada, Texas in the USA, or Saudi Arabia overseas. Others are found offshore underwater. The equipment found on land is also used offshore, but it is kept on large platforms either moored or floating above the underwater field. Those offshore platforms can be found in places like the North Sea near Scotland and Norway, the Gulf of Mexico near Texas in the USA, or north of Australia in the Timor Sea.

Transporting gas from these facilities can be done by underwater piping or by large ships with large tanks that are capable of holding gas under pressure, or large volumes of oil. Transport alone is a huge industry employing many well qualified and highly educated people.

Gas and oil are known as "fossil fuels" because they are produced by the natural decay of fossilized remains of animals and plants from millions of years ago deep in the ground. You can think of them as "dinosaur oil". Coal is another form of fossil fuel used in solid form and found nearer to the surface of the earth. Because coal is solid, it is mined not pumped. These are all non-renewable resources. Fossil fuels are found in abundance but there is only a finite amount. Once we use them up, they will be gone.

Humanity has been burning fossil fuels since fire was first discovered. It is convenient and fuels contain a lot of useful energy in an easily transportable form. We've been burning them in ever-increasing quantities as our population on the planet has grown historically, and as we industrialized. The ability to use steam to power machinery for factories and train engines occurred a few hundred years ago. The primary fuel was originally coal which was used to heat water to form steam to power engines. The coal also produced a lot of pollution as it was burned. The effects of that pollution were not well understood until recently. Today we know it is harmful to our atmosphere which is also limited, and to our own health. In some areas of the world coal has been phased out as a fuel because of its harmful effects.

When oil was discovered in large quantities it began to replace coal as the primary fuel because it contains more energy in a small space, and it is easier to store and transport. Like coal, it produces harmful by-products in the atmosphere, but not quite as bad as coal's. Replacing oil as a primary fuel is also being undertaken but more slowly as we are far more dependent on it. Oil is also easily transported so it is very good for mobile equipment, trucks, cars, trains, ships and planes.

Natural gas is cleaner burning, but it also produces some harmful gas by-products. None of these fuels is entirely "clean". Gas is more difficult to contain than liquid fuels and can be more dangerous when it leaks.

Extracting and using these fuels requires a great deal of effort and knowledge. Engineers, technicians and many others are needed. Also, a great deal of effort, knowledge and innovation goes into finding cleaner ways to use them so we do less harm to our atmosphere, but we haven't solved all the problems. There is a need for smart people like you with innovative ideas to help us get even cleaner.

In combination, these fuels have created a serious problem for our planet. By-products of burning them include carbon dioxide which is known as a greenhouse gas. In our atmosphere, it contributes to global warming which we know to be a big problem today.

The problems we have from burning fossil fuels have led to a lot of innovation, and we are now experiencing a growth in electrical automobiles and other means of electrified transport. We are generating power with nuclear energy in large power plants, solar power from panels, wind turbines in large windy areas, tidal waves in coastal areas, and hydroelectric dams that harness the energy of water as it flows downhill in mountainous areas.

There are plenty of opportunities in these industries to help in cleaning up the use of fuels and finding clean alternatives.

GETTING DRESSED

You've got out of bed, turned on the lights, had a shower and now you get dressed. Let's look at the clothes we wear.

Your clothes are probably bought in a store and in the store, you'll find a huge variety of options. Different articles like shirts, pants, skirts, underwear and socks. You'll find various brands – some expensive, some not so expensive. You'll find many different colors, styles and sizes.

Most clothing is made by people operating sewing machines in factories. Imagine a lot of people in a large room, each with a sewing machine, a nearby supply of material, buttons and thread. They are working on a pattern that was produced by a designer for the particular style and size that the worker produces on the sewing machine.

A lot of work goes into making any article of clothing. That's known as being "labor intensive". Because of that, a lot of clothing is produced overseas by workers in less well-developed countries who earn less than we do here in "Western" society. The finished clothing needs to be packaged and shipped to the companies that distribute and sell it to us in retail stores. The clothes that you put on today may come from several different countries and via different shipping routes. Your shirt may come from Malaysia, your pants from Indonesia, your shoes from China and your underwear from Mexico.

Some of it was shipped by truck, some by train, and some by ship. It may have travelled halfway around the world in a shipping container to a port on the coast of your country, then by train to a distribution center, by truck to your store and by car or bus from the store to your closet.

5 *Your clothes can travel a long way to get to you*

Those materials that your clothes are made of may be natural like cotton or wool, or synthetic (man-made) like polyester and nylon. Those man-made fibers come from dinosaur oil! Natural materials are fibers that grow on plants (cotton or flax), hair or skins of animals like sheep, lambs and cattle (leather). Your shoes are probably a combination of leather (from the skin of an animal), plastic or rubber (made from oil), and fabrics and threads that could be synthetic or natural. Those materials are delivered from their sources – usually farms or chemical plants, to the factory where the clothes are made. One factory may make the soles and heels for shoes, while another adds the leather or fabric uppers.

The last factory in the manufacturing process will package them for shipment, store them until they can be shipped, and then ship them away – perhaps to another warehouse for loading onto a ship.

Natural clothing fibers are farmed. Cotton and flax are plants that are processed to convert their fibers into threads that can be used in large looms to make large sheets of cloth. Those are shipped to factories where the cloth is cut into pieces to match a pattern and then sewed together with other pieces to form the final article. There could be a different pattern for each of the left and right sleeves, the back and front panels, and the collar and cuffs of a shirt.

Synthetic materials like nylon and polyester are also used. They are tough and durable, and they stretch a little. Polyester is often made into large sheets like cotton and flax. Nylon is used for its strength and durability. It is often used in strips to form elastics, or woven into the cloth with polyester to make the cloth stronger and more wear resistant.

Depending on the style and article of clothing it may also incorporate leather patches from the hides of animals, or have reinforcing plastic parts sewn into the elbows or shoulders or back panels like the protective jackets for motorcycling.

Clothes for different purposes will have special properties like quick drying for camping and sports clothing, stretch for yoga or dance, thermal insulation for cold weather use, and ultra-violet filtering for skin protection in very sunny areas. Each of those requires a different blend of properties that come from the different materials that are used. They may also be the result of chemical treatments to the materials or the clothing after it is manufactured. Chemical treatments can be used to make clothing fire-resistant, or to give it never-crease (non-iron) properties and of course for colors. Color is achieved by dyes that are also produced from either natural or synthetic sources.

High fashion clothes often come from countries with expensive labor and great designers! Often those clothes are made to fit the person who will wear them. Men's suits are often made or altered by tailors in the stores where they are bought. Some tailors start from scratch with bolts of materials that the customer can choose, or from an off-the-shelf suit made overseas and modified (tailored) to fit. Both men and women use tailored clothing – business suits, and party gowns. Wedding dresses are usually tailored specifically to fit the person who is buying them.

Even your clothes have a lot that's going on behind what you see and what you put on every day. Those long delivery "chains" are often known as "supply chains". If those are disrupted, the price of whatever is being shipped can be affected. If that ship from Indonesia with a container that has your shirt in it, has to go around Africa instead of through the Suez Canal, the ship will take longer to reach its destination and burn more fuel. That adds to the shipping cost and ultimately shows up as an increase in the price you pay.

COOKING YOUR BREAKFAST

One of your parents usually prepares breakfast for you. It might be a bowl of cereal and some juice, porridge, bacon and eggs or some other favorite for starting your day. If it's cooked, that was probably done in a microwave oven, or on a stove that is heated by electricity or natural gas. We've talked about how both electricity and gas get to your house, so let's look at the appliances – the microwave oven, and the stove, then we'll look at the food itself.

The microwave and stove are manufactured in factories, using combinations of materials that include oil products like rubber parts, and mined metals like sheet steel, copper wires, electronic circuit cards containing many parts made of many materials, and glass which comes from mined silica sand, soda ash and limestone. Those parts and materials were manufactured in their own factories from raw materials by skilled workers trained to make them.

Those parts were shipped to the factory that made the stove or microwave. They were made by skilled workers trained in that part of the manufacturing process, and probably a long way from where you live. Many manufactured goods are made in lower-cost locations overseas and shipped a long way to get to your home.

Getting them to your house was a lengthy transportation challenge, not unlike the clothes you are dressed in. They started at a factory, were loaded into containers, and shipped by truck, train, ship or some combination of those, to reach the store where your parents bought them. They may have carried the microwave home themselves, but the stove is big and may need special installation like the connection of gas lines and heavy-duty electrical wiring.

The installers are trained in the installation of your appliances, electrical circuits and gas piping in your house. They need to be trained to do that safely because both electricity and gas are dangerous to work with, and to you if they make mistakes. Training them requires additional schooling and practice beyond high school. In fact, many of the workers you see building houses, fixing cars, repairing traffic signals and wiring in the streets need that same type of training in the skills and specialized knowledge they will need to do their jobs safely and correctly.

How about the food? Where is it from?

Your parents shopped at a grocery store or market to bring your breakfast food to you. That food was also shipped by truck to the store from a "distribution center". It all started at a farm somewhere. Because food can spoil, it usually won't travel as far, nor as long, as appliances and clothing, but it still needs to travel.

For cereals, the bread used in your toast, butter, and milk, the food from the farms went to a processing plant where it was treated and cooked or converted into the final form you see at home. That butter started as milk from a cow in a barn. That milk was treated to make sure it was free of disease-causing bacteria. The cereal started as wheat or other grains, was ground to a powder, like flour, and then mixed with other ingredients to make the bread dough or uncooked cereals, it was then baked, cooled, and packaged for shipment to the store where your parents bought it.

Eggs came from chickens at farms, were collected carefully and shipped to distribution centers, and then to your store.

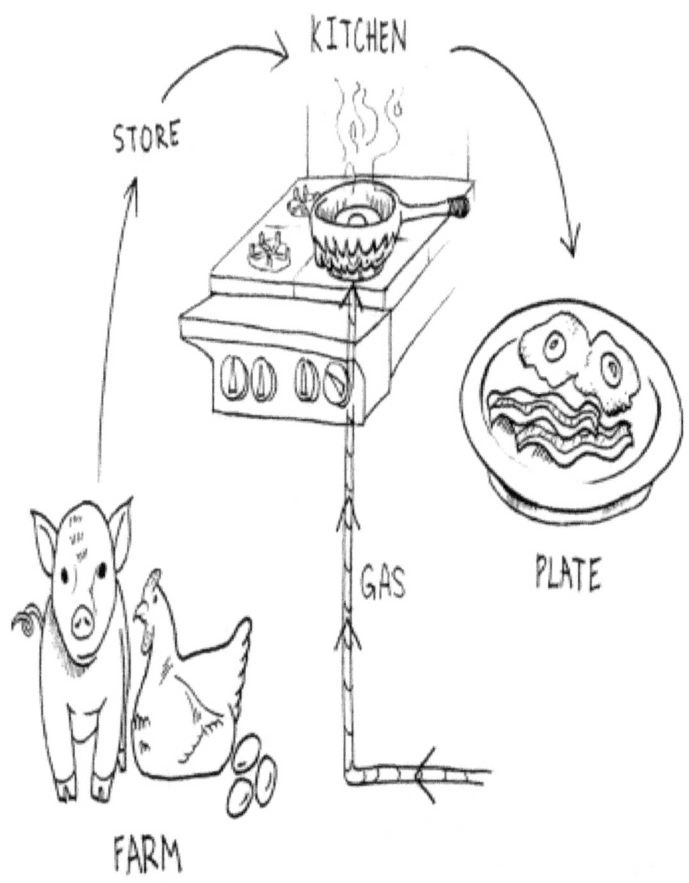

6 From farm to your kitchen

MEAT IS FROM LIVE ANIMALS like pigs, cattle, and chickens that are grown on farms. When they are old and big enough, they are taken away to a meat processing plant. They are killed in ways that don't cause them pain, then cut up into various cuts of meat. That bacon on your plate was once the belly of a pig in a field on a farm somewhere. Once cut into the desired shapes and pieces, the meat is packaged for sale, and shipped to the grocery store, then brought home for your meal

Making all those products takes very specialized equipment and skilled workers to do it right, and to make sure that the food doesn't get contaminated.

The machinery that is used has to be cleaned thoroughly and regularly to make sure it doesn't contaminate your food with bacteria or anything else that could make you sick. The people who do that cleaning need to be trained on how to do it safely and on how to make sure the equipment is free of contamination before it is used again.

Now, you have finished breakfast and the dishes need to be washed. You might put them in a dishwasher or a sink. They are washed using soap designed to remove the residue from cooked food and leave your dishes clean and sanitized. That soap is made in a chemical plant somewhere and designed specifically for that purpose. It is different from the soap and shampoo that you use in the shower and different from the soaps used to mop floors and clean ovens.

Those unique formulations of soap have different properties that are needed for their specific uses. In addition to the workers in the chemical plant who use their equipment to make these for you, there are chemists and engineers who develop the formulation of chemicals needed, how much of each, and how to actually mix them together properly to make the particular product. There's a lot of science involved in that formulation process. Again, those chemists, technicians, and engineers go through a lot of post-secondary education to learn how to do it. When it comes to food and some other chemicals, those workers may also be licensed to certify that they are both trained and competent.

The work they do is very interesting and they can be quite creative too. They use science like art to create some of the products you use. And, like many people who need a lot of education and training to do their jobs, they are usually quite well paid for their work.

GETTING TO SCHOOL

It's time to go to school. You might walk, but you also have alternatives. Your parents may drive you, you might ride your bicycle, skateboard or rollerblades, or take a school bus. All of those use manufactured products. Like the stove, piping, wires and food, also come from factories and workers who are trained to build the product.

Let's look at the school bus. It's big and designed to carry a lot of students. It drives around on a pre-determined route, stopping at pre-determined points to pick up its student riders. It is one of many busses all doing the same thing, at the same time, on different routes, stopping at different points, all with one purpose – to get you and your fellow students to school in time for classes to start for the day, and later, to get you home.

7 School bus, route and planning

The bus is manufactured and like other manufacturing, it contains materials from a variety of sources, many of them pre-manufactured into tires, windows, steering wheels, seats, doors and more. They come together at the bus factory where they are assembled in a pre-determined sequence to build the bus you ride.

All of those parts and the bus itself, are engineered to be strong enough to do their jobs safely, and to last a long time once they are put into use. Busses are expensive and unlike cars, much of the assembly is done by hand. There aren't enough of them to justify a fully automated assembly lines, like we find for cars. But, like the automated lines, the exact sequence and positioning of parts at the right times are needed. When they are put together, the right number of fasteners must be used and tightened so that nothing just falls apart.

Following those instructions and doing the assembly steps requires training and skill. Designing the whole process is another level of skill and knowledge – often done by engineers who are graduates of universities.

The driver is also a trained specialist. Because they are transporting people, and especially children, they are trained to drive very safely. They know how to avoid accidents and what to do to minimize the harm if they do get into an accident. They are also trained in how to inspect their bus every day so it is always safe. They follow that bus route and know exactly where to stop to pick you up and drop you off.

That route, its stops, and its timing are all determined by planners. Planners know what it takes to drive the bus route and how long it should take for each part of the journey and each stop. They know how many students should be getting on at each of those stops. The driver must follow the route, or you could be waiting extra-long for him, or he could get there too early and you'd miss the bus entirely!

The driver and the planner for the route work for companies hired by the school board. The school board is paid for by your local government and they get their money from taxes. We'll talk about government later, but for your trip to school, you can see now that there is a lot involved – the bus, the route, the stops, careful planning, training of the driver and the actual driving. Like many of the things and services we encounter every day, there's a lot that goes into making it happen smoothly!

KEEPING THE CLASSROOM WARM IN WINTER, COOL IN SUMMER

We all work and learn best when we are comfortable. If we are too hot or too cold, our minds pay attention to our discomfort and ignore what we are there to do. In school, that means we don't learn well. Parents make sure you have clothes and are dressed for the season. You might wear shorts or skirts in summer and heavy coats with boots in winter.

8 School - a comfortable place to learn

DEPENDING ON WHERE you live, whether it is often hot or cold outside, your school may have heating and air conditioning. Schools are usually pretty big so heating and air conditioning have to work in a large space with many rooms. Sometimes windows and doors will be open, and the air inside needs to be kept fresh. Heating and air conditioning are built as "systems". A system is a set of things that are connected together to do some job for us – like heating.

In the heating system, there is a furnace to burn fuel or convert electrical energy into heat. That heat needs to be cooled off from furnace temperatures or we will get burned. That happens when a big volume of air is blown across a hot surface inside the furnace. The hot gas from combustion is on one side of the surface. The cooler air is on the other side. As the cool air passes the hot surface, it picks up heat and is blown through the ducting to the rooms in the building. Sometimes water is used instead of air. It is also heated and piped to radiators in the various rooms.

Hot air mixes with cool air in your room to warm it up. Hot water heats the radiator and it heats the air around it. When the room reaches a comfortable temperature, a sensor, known as a thermostat, shuts off the supply of warm water or air so that the room isn't overheated.

The same sort of system carries cooling air or water to your room in hot weather. Instead of a furnace, there is an air conditioning unit or chiller. It cools a liquid and gas mixture known as a refrigerant. The refrigerant is piped to a cooler where it absorbs heat, cooling the air in your room.

Those systems of pipes and air ducts are made of metals. The chiller, air conditioning unit, and furnace are built with metals. Furnaces burn fuel. Air conditioners are electric. The refrigerant they use is a chemical fluid. That equipment all comes from mines and minerals in the earth. The refrigerant comes from a variety of chemicals, supplied by a chemical plant. The chemical plant gets its supplies from other chemical producers, mines, oil, gas and electric utilities.

A lot of people are involved in making all that equipment, mining and transporting the materials used in its manufacture. Likewise, for the refrigerant – a lot of people and knowledge are involved in getting that finished product ready for use in your school's air conditioner.

The knowledge of how to build those systems and produce those metals and chemicals requires a good deal of education. Many people who work in those fields have college educations and some, like engineers, whose decisions can affect your safety, are licensed to ensure they are both knowledgeable and competent to do their jobs.

READING, i-PAD (TABLETS), COMPUTERS AND CELL PHONES

In school, you are a part of a class. It has other children who are around your age and all learning the same subjects. As you learn more, the subjects become progressively more detailed and complex. The further you go in school, the of what you learn will be needed in everyday life. If you progress to college or university or into a skilled trade, you will learn very specialized knowledge that is needed in your field of study and eventually in your chosen career.

Engineers have been mentioned. To design machines, and systems, chemical processes to build buildings, bridges and big equipment, engineers require a lot of technical knowledge. They are usually very good at math and science. They learn what science teaches and then apply it to real-world problems. Engineers are terrific problem solvers when it comes to technical problems and challenges. Things you see every day, like cars, buses, your school building, airplanes in the sky, machines that load and unload trucks, and so much more, are all designed by engineers. The piping and heating duct systems, the electrical systems that deliver power to your plug, are all "hidden" from view, and they are designed by engineers.

The mechanics that fix your parents' car, the road crews working on your city streets, the electricians working on traffic lights, and the people who build new homes and larger buildings, all have special knowledge and skills. They know what to do, and how to do it. Without them you wouldn't get to school, there would be no road, and you wouldn't enjoy a comfortable atmosphere in the building, have lights for reading, and so much more.

All that education is taught in schools, colleges and universities. Some jobs require a lot of education – like doctors, dentists, nurses, engineers, scientists, and even teachers. Some require a little less education but more hands-on practical learning like electricians, mechanics, lab and other technicians.

9 Plenty of devices and the jobs that make them, all need an education

They all learn their basics, and their higher education and skills in schools, colleges or academies. To learn they need teachers who know those skills and knowledge, who can explain the concepts they need to know, and to provide guidance on how to do it. The knowledge is usually available in books or computer systems. It can be read, listened to in presentations or radio, or watched like on TV or social media.

Books are produced with paper and ink, glues and other binding materials to hold them together. The paper comes from a big paper-making factory, the printing is done in large high-speed presses and the binding is put together by machines.

The paper can actually be re-used and recycled when we are done with it. When trees are cut down to make paper they are replaced with young saplings. Forests and new growth are great ways to capture a major pollutant in our atmosphere – carbon.

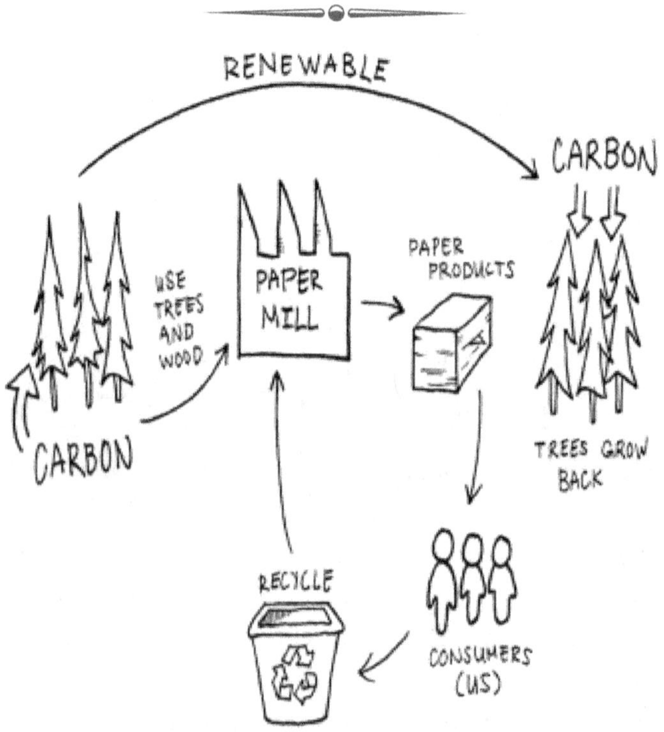

10 You are part of the cycle recycling renewable and reusable resources

OUR WORLD

THE I-PAD (TABLET) and computers you use, like mobile phones, are made of electronic components. So are the gaming consoles and electronics you use at home. They operate on the same basic scientific principles and are made in factories that are all similar but produce different products.

The components they are made of, are usually simple but highly engineered devices, that are combined in systems to produce the sound or video you use. Those devices are often made of special, exotic materials, like copper for conductors, rare earths for diodes, transistors, silica for computer chips, lithium and other metals for batteries. Each of those comes from a factory somewhere, and those factories are supplied by other factories and with materials that are processed from mined substances in the earth.

There is a huge amount of research, design and engineering that goes into all those products. And behind that is a lot of education and learning.

Someday you might want to be an engineer, or a designer, or a scientist. You will need a good education so you want to do well in school to prepare yourself. The colleges they go to can be picky about who they select as students. Unlike primary and secondary schools, they don't accept everyone. You need to want to be there. You need to want what they teach. You must be motivated as well as smart. Your parents may even want to help you achieve those high marks. High marks in school show that you are both smart and motivated to learn.

If you want to do well in life, you will want to have a well-paying job. Those jobs and many more like technicians, teachers, college professors, tradespersons, bankers, store managers, nurses, doctors, dentists, police, fire and ambulance workers are all well paid and well educated. Most of the jobs you might find interesting require some higher education and skills, some more than others.

SHOPPING AND HOW MONEY WORKS

Your food, clothes, school supplies, the furniture in your home, and just about everything else we use in some way, are purchased from a store. Even if your dad makes his own furniture, he buys the wood from a lumber or building supply store. All of those stores, get their products from other suppliers who usually sell to many stores. Those are called distributors because they distribute goods to other suppliers, or wholesalers because they sell at reduced or "wholesale" pricing because of the large volume of products they sell. All of their supplies come from manufacturers as we've talked about before.

Have you ever thought much about the money that is used to make those purchases?

In the past, long ago, people didn't use money. They would trade goods or services. They might exchange firewood that they've cut and dried, for food or clothing that someone else has made or prepared. That is known as a "barter" system. Of course, it is awkward to carry around firewood or food to use whenever you want to barter for something from someone else. You may also find that the person you want something from doesn't need your firewood. Then what do you do?

Money was invented to represent the value that the firewood and food have to a potential user or "buyer". Money can be exchanged for your firewood, and you can then use the money to acquire whatever you want. The person you buy from no longer needs to have a use for your firewood.

11 From barter (trading) to money

Anything can be used as money. Cattle, shells, beads, coins and paper have all been used throughout history. Today we use mainly coin and paper money or we "promise" to pay using credit cards or other forms of "promissory notes".

Money represents value to its users. It has a "face value" in your local currency – dollars or whatever currency is used in your country. The actual paper it is printed on has very little value, but it represents value and can be exchanged for goods or services. Money is usually minted (coins) or printed (bank notes) by governments. Some governments use the money to represent an amount of gold that is stored in safe locations or vaults, others use money to represent the amount of debt they are prepared to repay. Fake money has no such backing so it does not represent any value at all. The supply of real money is controlled by the government so that it continues to represent value to its users.

Real money is also difficult to copy. That makes it difficult to cheat the system by making your own fake, or counterfeit, money. Fake money reduces the value of all the money that is provided because it has no real value. Making it or using it can get you thrown in jail!

Money has been in use for thousands of years. It replaces barter systems and it has worked very well. Most countries have their own forms of money. Each form is called a "currency" and they are different from country to country. Some, like Canada and the USA, use dollars. Mexico has its Pesos. Spain has its Pesos. In Europe they use Euros. In Japan they use Yen. Although those are all different currencies, they all represent value. The amount of value represented by one, compared with another is known as an "exchange" rate. For example, one US dollar might be worth 0.93 Euro, or 1.37 Canadian dollars. They can all be used to buy the same goods or services in the areas where they are used.

A loaf of bread might cost 3 Canadian dollars in Canada, or 2.2 US dollars in the USA, but it is still one loaf of bread with the same "value" in all three places.

When you go shopping, you will exchange your local currency for goods or services that have a value represented by that currency. The store owner can then exchange the currency you paid to him, to pay his employees. They can then buy what they need from the stores of their choosing.

GETTING SICK AND BETTER AGAIN

The human body, which we all have, is not much different from those of animals in the wild, except that it looks different. All animals, including us, have digestive systems, nervous systems, brains, ways of moving ourselves around (legs, wings, feet, flippers), etc. Those various systems we have all work together in our body and there are a large number of problems we can have that reduce our ability to do what we want.

We all get sick from time to time. We might get a cold or a flu, or we might break an arm or leg. Sometimes we have serious illnesses that can be life-threatening like cancer or heart problems.

As humans, we have developed "health care" to help us when we get sick. Health care involves taking care of ourselves so we don't get sick. It involves eating well so we maintain good conditions for our bodies internally. And it involves taking medicines or having physical help when we need it.

Animals in the wild don't have that, and only our pets and farm animals get a form of health care from veterinarians.

As we grow up, we grow physically. That growth is enabled by the food we eat, so in a very real way, we are what we eat. If we eat good healthy foods, our bodies will grow up to be healthy. If we eat a lot of junk food or don't eat enough, we will not be as healthy. When we are healthy, we feel good and we can do whatever we want within the limits of what a human body can do. We can run, walk, throw, catch, skate, ski, talk, shout, sing, etc. The healthier we are, the more we can do. If we are unhealthy, we might find it difficult to run, climb, walk long distances, or even breathe.

Being unhealthy will shorten your life too. Healthy people can live long lives. Unhealthy people catch more diseases and are prone to dying younger. Unfortunately, some people are born with genetic defects and conditions that can be very difficult to live with. You want to be as healthy as you can so that you can enjoy your life to the fullest, and live long!

Anyone can be hurt in an accident – break an arm, or a leg, damage internal organs like our stomach, or liver. When that happens, sometimes our bodies can heal themselves, but not always. We may need help to fix it. We might need surgery or the setting of broken bones. We can also get sick from eating poisons or chemicals that are harmful to our bodies. If we are sick, we can sometimes heal ourselves, or we may need help in the form of medicines. In some cases, we may not be able to get rid of the substance that harmed us and we remain sick.

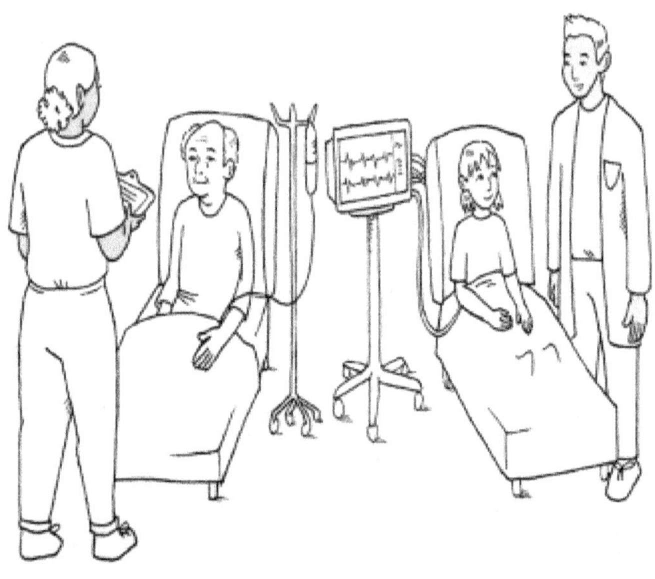

12 Hospitals help us when we are sick or hurt

WE KNOW WHAT FOODS are good for us and we know what foods can harm us. We know that some chemicals are harmless while others are harmful. But sometimes harmful substances are used in food that is normally considered to be good for us. To help grow enough food, farmers will use insecticides and other chemicals on the food they grow. Those chemicals end up in the food they sell and eventually make their way into our bodies. Some are more harmful than others. We accept this because having enough food for everyone is considered to be a good thing, even if that food is not as healthy as it should be. We can buy chemical-free foods – known as organic, or we can buy food that is contaminated in small quantities. The choice is ours when we shop.

Organic foods are usually expensive, so if you want to eat them, you want to find a good paying job. The choices you make now while you are still in school can help you achieve that.

Growing organic foods means that insects and other diseases that can affect crops and farm animals must be dealt with without the use of chemicals. That requires labor and that labor can be more expensive than the chemicals. To save money, chemicals are often used and organic foods are often more expensive. If we don't have enough money for organic food, we have little option but to buy the cheaper and more risky alternatives. We may later suffer health consequences too, and pay for it in health care costs.

We don't always know what harm all of these chemicals in our food can do. In some cases, we have discovered the harm and stopped using the chemicals. In other cases, we continue to use it because we don't know for sure it is harmful. It might be doing good, or it might be doing harm. Sadly, not everyone in business cares about everyone's health. In business, it is all about making money, not keeping us healthy. Businesses consider that unless something is proven to be harmful it is assumed to be harmless. They want your money more than your health.

Eating good quality foods to stay healthy, or trusting that chemicals are harmless, is a choice we all need to make.

If we get sick, we may need to use our health care system. Not all countries have the same sort of health care. In Canada, the government pays for health care to fix problems. It gets the money for that from taxes. In the USA, the government doesn't pay for all the needed health care – it is up to the individuals who often use insurance companies because health care costs can be high. Some countries are poor and do not have any health care systems at all. In those countries, if you can't pay for health care and you need it, you are out of luck. You will stay sick and possibly even die.

In most developed countries there is some form of health care system. Many involve the government in paying for it so that it is accessible to everyone. A few, like the USA, don't do that. They have excellent health care facilities and workers, but it is up to the individual to pay directly. If they've got the money, they can get the best health care available, but if they don't have the money, they may suffer.

Regardless of how it is paid for, a health care system is usually focused on correcting problems that occur. They work like an automotive garage to fix your car when it breaks down. They do very little to help you avoid getting sick or injured beyond education in what to do to live a healthy life style.

Good food, enough food, the right mix of foods, regular exercise and avoidance of some harmful substances like smoking and alcohol, all contribute to good health. Unless your body has some problems that you inherited from your parents (like a weak heart, or poor digestion), you can play a big role in your own health. If you have problems though, you can turn to the health care system for help.

Health care is what you do to avoid being sick or injured. Living a healthy life style does not guarantee you won't get sick though. Some diseases occur even in the healthiest of people. "Sick care" is what the doctors and nurses do in their hospitals to help you recover from disease or injury.

Some people might be offended by calling it a "sick care" system, but if you visit a hospital, you will see what I mean. Hospitals are mostly full of sick people. Some are also there to care for injuries. Doctors treat mostly sicknesses and injuries once they have occurred. They can do little to help us remain healthy once we are out of their care. That is up to us.

Doctors and nurses will help you when you get sick or injured. Doing so requires a lot of knowledge and skill. They go to school for a long time to study medicine and nursing. Some specialize in healing specific problems. There are heart doctors (cardiologists), bone doctors (orthopedic doctors), brain doctors (neurosurgeons), digestive system doctors (gastric specialists), reproductive system doctors, and so on. The health care professions have many specialties related to specific parts of our bodies or to specific diseases like cancer or mental illnesses.

Doctors and other health care professionals tend to be well-paid and well-regarded by society. They do a lot of good for people who are truly in need of help.

In addition to the doctors, nurses and hospitals that fix us, and that governments often pay for, other medical professionals help us stay healthy. They help us stay out of hospitals and they help us recover after surgeries.

Some doctors and therapists often work outside the formal government-funded healthcare systems. There are physiotherapists who help us recover when our bodies have suffered from physical trauma. There are sports therapists to help us with the injuries and challenges we subject ourselves to through over-exertion in sports. Massage therapists help our muscles when they are over used or hurt. Chiropractors help us to keep our spines in the correct curved shape and keep our central nervous system functioning as it should. Naturopathic doctors help us to prevent and correct a wide range of ailments that the formal medical system doesn't yet consider serious enough to be "sick" and require their sick care.

There are mental health professionals – doctors or psychiatrists, who often use drugs to treat mental disorders that are often not curable. There are psychotherapists who help us deal with mental troubles that aren't usually considered to be illnesses, but they are conditions that we need help to treat. They might help someone dealing with the trauma or grief of losing a loved one or recovering from abuse, struggling to get along with a spouse, or even struggling with their own identity. There are many conditions that can bother us that we may need help with.

These are not exhaustive lists of medical and health care professionals. They are all valuable members of our society with a high level of education and dedication to doing what they can to help us.

There is also a large industry that provides medicines, drugs and other substances that are used to help us and our doctors. The pharmaceutical industry produces the drugs that doctors often use to help with pain, treat a wide variety of conditions, help us sleep, help us digest food better, help us calm down, and so on. Pharmaceutical drugs can be very powerful and harmful if used in excess. The products they make can therefore harm us if used incorrectly, so to use them, we usually need a doctor to prescribe them for us.

Often those drugs are also very expensive. They take a long time to discover and develop and the companies that produce them, need to recover their costs, or they might go out of business. If that happens, we'd all suffer, so we accept the higher costs of their specialized and sometimes lifesaving products.

There is also a wide range of natural substances that can be used to supplement our diets. Because of the large-scale farming used to feed so many of us, the soil is often tired but it must keep growing food. It is helped with fertilizers and some minerals, but often the food itself will be lacking in all the minerals and vitamins we need. There are also companies that produce natural food supplements and vitamins. Sometimes pharmaceutical companies produce those and sometimes other companies specialize in natural health support products. Those natural products don't require prescriptions and we can buy them easily. They can also be expensive, but not as expensive as pharmaceutical drugs. They are optional, and some people never use them. Others use them extensively. The choice is always yours to enhance your health or to rely on your body alone without helping it.

68

WHAT HAPPENS WHEN SOMETHING BREAKS?

The health care professions and hospitals are there to help us stay healthy and to get healthy once we get sick or something hurts us. Although there isn't an organized system like health care for the infrastructure and equipment we use, there are people who look after it. Those are maintainers.

Cities look after their roads and traffic signals. Companies and governments look after their buildings. Heating systems and air conditioning systems can all break down. Cars, trucks, and motorcycles can all break down. Factories and large industrial plants can also break down. At home, our heating system, dishwasher, stove or refrigerator can break down. Lights burn out, door bells stop working, and windows get dirty. Our phone networks and the internet can be down. In fact, anything we can design and build can stop doing what it is supposed to do. It can perform at a lower standard, or it can break down altogether. Nothing truly lasts forever.

Taking care of these things we have and use is known as maintenance, fixing them when they break is called repair. Like we have health care and sick care for our bodies and minds, we also have maintenance programs and repairs for our physical systems.

The simplest form of maintenance is to do nothing until the item breaks, then replace it or repair it. Some things are small and expendable so we simply replace them. Lighting in our homes is a good example. We use it until it stops, and then we change the bulb or element. Cars are more expensive and they have many more complicated ways of not working. We don't just throw them away and replace them when they stop doing what we want. We take care of them with oil and filter changes, keeping brake fluid topped up, keeping washer fluid in the windshield washer reservoir, changing tires before they wear out and keeping it clean so we don't mind being seen in it.

13 Things break and need maintenance

THOSE ARE ALL EXAMPLES of maintenance. We don't always need to wait until something breaks to do something that will keep it working well. In fact, most things that can break or stop working can be maintained so that they don't. That effort to maintain helps us avoid the bad that can happen when the breakdown occurs and the avoidance of that inconvenience or loss of capability that we depend on, makes the effort to maintain worth doing.

Many don't think much about maintenance. We know that it exists because we have a custodian who changes lights, cleans the floors, and fixes the heating in our schools. That sort of effort is required at home, in churches, in factories, in office buildings, and even outside in our parks and on our roadways.

A good maintenance program requires thought about what can break down, why it breaks down, and whether or not there is something that can be done about it before it breaks down. We cannot prevent a light bulb from burning out, but we can prevent our car engine from being damaged by dirt in its oil. We can't prevent a tree from falling on overhead wires in high winds, but we can trim the tree so it is less likely to fall and so it does less damage if it happens. We can't prevent dirt from accumulating on windows and signs, but we can clean it off periodically to make sure we can see through the windows clearly and read the signs.

When things break, they disrupt whatever they are doing. If the electric wires to your house break in a storm, they cause your lights to go out, your TV and internet to stop, heating or air conditioning to stop and they prevent you from cooking. That is disruptive to your family and its way of life. The high wind in a storm cannot be prevented but the wires can be maintained so that they are securely attached to their poles so that their connections with other wires and electrical equipment are tight and secure, and so that the insulation on the wires is in good condition. We expect our electric utility company to take good care of its equipment and wiring and we are paying them for it. We are paying for maintenance because we don't want the disruption that happens when their equipment breaks.

Different equipment and systems have different consequences when they break. If a hammer breaks while you are using it to nail wood together, you can easily replace the hammer. You may not pay much attention to it until it breaks, and it is not expensive to replace. If the rain gutters on your house are plugged with leaves and other debris, they do not channel rainwater where it should go and can cause leaking inside your house. That leakage can damage woodwork and walls. It is expensive to fix. A little bit of maintenance, cleaning out the gutters, can avoid all that. In that case, the maintenance, which is nothing more than climbing a ladder to clean the gutter, is worth doing.

Cleaning the gutters is proactive – it is done to avoid the consequences of the problem that arise if you don't do it. Repairing woodwork and walls is a repair. Repairs are reactive to what has already happened. When you are doing repairs, you are also living with whatever consequences arise from not being proactive. It will surely be more expensive and far more disruptive to your lifestyle in the house than a little bit of time invested in cleaning gutters.

Maintenance is rarely a career choice because it is simply not well known. It is not taught by many schools, and none of them are in North America. Many engineers get into it because they work in plants where it is needed and they get involved in helping to solve problems. Reliability is also a challenge to find, yet it is widely needed. Some get into it through maintenance, and others take postgraduate-level courses in reliability, but only a few universities in the world actually offer that.

Despite all that, it is a field that many who find themselves in it, also truly love it. It is both challenging with lots of problem-solving, and rewarding when it all works out. The author of this book is one of them!

HELP IS THERE WHEN YOU NEED IT

You've seen fire trucks, police cars, ambulances, tow trucks and emergency repair vehicles. They are there when something goes wrong. The vehicles themselves are specialized for their work and the people who operate them are trained on how to use them, and in some cases how to help people in distress. Police, fire and ambulance staff can all help injured people or those who might be suffering sudden ailments like heart attacks. They all need extensive training in their own field as well as how to respond when people are in emergencies and in need of help.

Police take training in the law and how to enforce it. They learn about small arms and how to perform tasks like arresting someone, without getting hurt themselves. They are taught how to deal with crowds, how to investigate crimes, and how to interrogate criminals. They learn a lot about the laws they are there to enforce and how to be good ambassadors for their cities.

Firefighters learn how to fight the different kinds of fire so that they don't make things worse by using the wrong techniques. They learn how to rescue people from burning and smoke-filled buildings. They also learn a lot about how to prevent fires and how to educate people on how to avoid them. In fact, most of their time is spent in the prevention and education of others, not in actually dealing with burning buildings.

Ambulance workers are highly trained medical professionals. They can do some procedures that doctors and nurses are not allowed to do. They learn how to save lives in difficult and often dangerous situations.

14 Help is there when you need it

Municipalities and utilities have response vehicles for emergency repair work. Repairing fallen electric power lines, leaking underground gas lines, and telecommunications towers damaged in storms is dangerous work and requires a great deal of skill as well as care.

When we get into a dangerous situation like an accident, we can call a number, often 911, and get help. One call will bring police, fire and ambulance services as needed. The person on the other end of the call knows how to ask the right questions to find out where you are, what happened, what problems you might be suffering from, and they know how to calm you down if you are upset or anxious. They know how to find the closest emergency service responders and dispatch them quickly to reach you, often within minutes. They can inform those emergency responders what they are about to find so they can be prepared to deliver what is often life-saving care as soon as they arrive.

All of that is organized and coordinated by municipalities to help their citizens when things go wrong. It's one of the many things that our cities and towns do for us that we often don't think about until we really need them. Just imagine what life would be like without them!

These careers and the work are well regarded and these skills are gained through a lot of education training and practice. These folks don't practice until they get it right, they practice like true professionals, so that they can't get it wrong!

GOVERNMENT-RUN BUSINESSES

(**P**OLICE, FIRE, AMBULANCE, HOSPITALS, SCHOOLS)

Emergency services are run by our local governments, but there are also other levels of government that provide more services. Our national government makes sure we have a military to keep our country from attack by others and to help our friends or allies when they need it. In the far north of Canada, we have the Canadian Rangers, a branch of the military reserve who live and work there, ensuring we have a national presence in those far off regions. Allies like Canada, the USA, Britain and many other European countries all work together to ensure there is a low risk of a major war in the entire North Atlantic region. By being well prepared for the worst, they actually help to avoid it.

Military and its work are often not seen in your day-to-day travels unless you live near a military base. The Army, Navy and Air Force all have jobs to do in the event of war, and they are always ready if needed. There are many challenging and rewarding careers in the military like vehicle mechanics, aircraft mechanics, electronics technicians, weapons technicians, navigation, ship operations, marine engineering, military civil engineering, aircraft engineering, cooks, nurses, doctors, and many more. In fact, the military is a great place to learn many trades and skills that are very useful outside of the military. Most military personnel do not remain in the military for their entire careers, so they learn how to do a job and do it well, then leave and get into some very good jobs as civilians.

The military experience is actually very rewarding for those who have done it. In most of the world, the actual risk of going to war is quite small, so being in the military doesn't increase your chances of being in a war at all. Even those who complete entire careers in the military, don't usually go to war. The lifestyle is quite structured and well-organized, and the friendships that people make in the military often last a lifetime.

15 Government is there for us

National governments also provide services like taxation, coast guard and aids to navigation, immigration and foreign affairs, international transport, airports and seaports, and they provide for the nation's highest level of law enforcement and judges for the Supreme Court. Governments are run by civil servants, professionals who run the many services and departments. They are answerable to our elected officials who are more like part-timers when it comes to actually running the workings of our country. Our elected officials are usually very smart people, who accept lower pay than they could get in industry. They are motivated and truly care about doing their best for their country and its people (us).

Countries often have states or provinces that handle other duties like providing education, roads, internal transportation like rail and regional air travel, policing and judicial services at the state or provincial level, and administering the entire health care system.

Municipalities are where we live and they often handle local roads, traffic signals, parks, recreation facilities, garbage and recycling, water distribution and wastewater treatment.

Government work can be very rewarding and the jobs tend to be very secure. Companies might lay off employees in tough times, but governments rarely do that. It is possible to work for the government, earn a good but usually not extravagant wage, and then retire comfortably. Governments may not pay the best, but they are good employers with benefits and pension plans that are hard to beat.

A very visible feature of government at all levels is the politicians who are elected as your representatives to run things. They actually don't do much of the day-to-day running of departments, but they do make sure it happens. The senior-level civil servants are the ones who actually run things. Elected officials make sure they run them as intended. They also make the laws we must all follow. They decide what laws are needed, or no longer needed, and then what to do about them. They draft the text of those laws, debate it in parliament and either approve or disapprove them.

All of the laws that govern how we interact in society are the product of the processes which is carried out by our elected officials.

ARE COLLEGE AND UNIVERSITY WORTH IT?

In grade school, you really don't need to think much about college or university, but when thinking of what career options you are attracted to, it's worth a little bit of thought.

Having a post-secondary education does open the door to many opportunities. Many jobs, career options and all professions require some level of college or university education. At the very least, when you get into high school, it is worthwhile to work on having good grades. Even if you don't eventually choose to go to on, good grades will keep that door open for you. With low grades, your options will be limited and the pay you can get is likely to be disappointing.

College opens up many practical career opportunities, many of which bring higher pay. The college experience can be personally and intellectually rewarding. University tends to be more academic than college, there are a number of professional career options there, and it can be very rewarding.

You will learn new ways of looking at things, critical thinking can help you see both sides of any situation, argument, offer or opportunity. Your communication skills will grow, making it easier for you to handle job interviews and in your future job performance where communication with co-workers, your bosses, and your customers, is always important.

OUR WORLD

In college and university, you can also be exposed to a variety of subjects that you don't get in grade school or high school. Many of those are quite interesting and can lead to exciting careers that we haven't even touched on in this book.

You will also make friends who come from further away than your own neighborhood, and be exposed to different cultural influences, languages and perspectives. College and university are both very good for developing a well-rounded perspective on life and living that isn't usually achieved in high school alone.

16 Education helps you get far in life

On the downside, college is not cheap, and university can be downright expensive! Even with government subsidies and scholarships where they exist, it can be expensive. Unless you come from a wealthy background, students often leave their post-secondary education laden with a substantial debt, a student loan, to be repaid.

That happens at that point in life where they are just beginning a new career, they want to save for a home, they might be thinking of starting a family, and now they have a big debt to repay. There are scholarships for the smartest students to help them with costs, as well as other forms of financial help but neither college or university comes without its financial burdens.

When it comes time to consider college and university, one thing that helps a lot, will be your grades. Scholarships are typically given for high scholastic achievement, and sometimes for sports.

What about being in a trade versus a profession? For trades you'll go to college, for professions, university. The professions require more education and are more difficult academically, to get into. That extra education takes one or two years longer, so it adds to your student debt obligations later. On the plus side, it is often offset by the higher earning potential of many professions. For instance, doctors, dentists and engineers can often make quite a bit more than therapists, hygienists, and technicians.

Another consideration will be future job stability. Right now, while you are in school, your parents take care of this for you. But, when you leave home, it becomes yours.

Professions and trades both offer fairly stable futures, some more stable than others if you are specialized. Trades are usually very stable in maintenance, construction, mechanical, plumbing and electrical fields. Professions with a lot of stability include law, medicine and dentistry. Both trades and professions can be turned into businesses that you run yourself too. Being an entrepreneur or business owner brings a lot of rewards and can be very satisfying, but it also brings some risk.

The primary consideration here will be your interests. In life, we always do best when we are doing the things we like. Don't make money or job stability how soon you can get out to work is your primary goal. Make your passion your goal and you will be on the right path, whatever it turns out to be.

EPILOGUE

In the chapters of this book, you've stepped through activities, or things you might see while living day to day. There is much in life and living that we take for granted – we assume it just "is" and seldom do many of us question how it came to be. There is often a long and convoluted path taken by many materials, goods, and services, to provide what we see as commonplace.

Most of us want to live full and meaningful lives with our basics taken care of and in some degree of comfort. We want to do something we love and if we can find that, we will truly thrive while doing it. But what is that thing we will love?

In some cases, you may already know – it may be music, sports, or gaming. How do you make a career out of those so you can do what you love, and get paid for it?

ASK LOTS OF ?

? QUESTIONS

your life, your choice!

Explore Your Options.

17 Be curious

IN OTHER CASES, SOME of you may not yet know. How do you find out? You see a lot during your day and behind most of what you see is a lot of depth. By asking questions about what is there, and how it got there, you find a number of different activities and with those, you'll find career opportunities. Some of those won't interest you, but others may.

You may not care now, but as you progress further in life, you may begin to care. At some point, you'll want to do something you enjoy. This book may serve to give you ideas. If not, it may spark some curiosity to go and find out. The world is full of many things that we'll never fully understand if we don't ask questions. That is what this book is trying to achieve - curiosity.

When you look at your bicycle, your cell phone, your gaming console, or your nice home-cooked meal, ask questions about it, and you can begin to see the rich complexity of our world as it is.

We want, indeed need, the world to be environmentally safe for us and our future children. It's easy to point fingers at industry and blame it for polluting and failing to clean up. But it is also important to realize that those industries we might think poorly of, are actually doing what they do in response to our personal choices.

For instance, most of us choose to use cell phones. Those require a variety of materials from many sources. They require complex mining and processing and then manufacture. If we stop using cell phones, some of those industries go away. With them go the jobs and the livelihoods of the families of their workers. But are you ready to give up that cell phone?

We want cell phones to be affordable. Everyone involved in delivering them to you, the salesperson in the store, the supplier to the store, the phone manufacturer, their suppliers, and their sources of raw materials, all need to participate in keeping costs down. The industries that supply the products that go into the cell phone need to be using environmentally friendly and healthy practices, and keep costs down. All of what they do now, and in the future is in response to what we, the consumers of those products are asking for.

Few of us really think about that. Environmental protesters use cell phones, wear jackets made of plastics (oil products) and get to their protests in cars, and busses that burn oil. Our life style is all done subconsciously, and it causes decisions about how to provide what we want. Whenever we look for a cheaper alternative, we are encouraging the seller and manufacturer to leave something out.

Just as organic food costs more than non-organic, green products often cost more too.

This book isn't about getting you to spend more on what you want, but it is hoped that in addition to making you more aware of what is out there, you will also become more aware of the impact your personal choices can have on all of us. I hope that enough questions have been asked, some answered, and that it encourages you to have greater curiosity about everything.

GLOSSARY

A few terms used in the book may be unfamiliar. Those are explained briefly here.

Barter: A system of exchange between two people, where each one trades something he or she has, for what the other has.

Chemicals: Basic elements which often combine with each other, from which everything we know is formed. Carbon, oxygen, and hydrogen are three common chemicals. When they combine, they form many organic substances like plant fibers, wood, and paper.

Chemical Reaction: A process that combines various chemicals to form new chemicals.

Chemical Reactor: A container in which a chemical reaction occurs.

Conductor: A material that is used to conduct, or transport, electricity. The electricity moves through the conductor.

Contaminants: Particles or chemicals that can spoil whatever they are in or on. Bacteria can contaminate drinking water.

Currency: A generic name for money from any country. The USD is a currency used in the USA. The Peso is a currency used in Mexico.

Distribution: To deliver something like electricity to many customers in the same area. A distribution system has wires to get electricity to all the houses in your neighborhood.

Exchange rate: A ratio of one currency relative to another where both express the same value. If a loaf of bread is worth $3 Canadian, and $2.2 US, then the exchange rate is $3/$2.2 = 1.36. It means that 1 USD is worth 1.36 times the value of 1 CAD.

Extraction: A process of separating one solid chemical material from another. We "extract" copper, gold and other metals from rocks that contain them naturally.

Flammable: Something that can burn easily is flammable.

Fossil fuels: These are fuels such as coal, oil, and natural gas that are created from the decay of plant and animal matter in the ground, after it dies.

Generation: A process of making large amounts of electricity using magnetic fields in a generator.

Insulator: In electrical systems, this is a material that does NOT conduct electricity. We use insulators to protect us from electric shock.

Interest: In finance, this is an amount of money paid to a lender, when you borrow money. It is added to the repayment of the original loan as a form of payment in return for being allowed to borrow.

Maintain: To keep something in or near a good condition so it can be used.

Maintenance: The work we do to maintain something.

Mercaptan: A very smelly chemical, even in small quantities. Natural gas is colorless and odorless, so Mercaptan is added to it so we can detect when it leaks.

Promissory Note: A written promise to pay a debt. If a person borrows from another, they promise to repay the debt in a certain time period and usually with some additional payment of interest.

Renewable: Something that does not disappear when used, regrows, or regenerates naturally is renewable. Wind and solar power a renewable because we cannot exhaust them. Coal and oil are non-renewable because they are only available in limited quantities, and when they are used up, they are gone for good.

Transistor: One of many different electronic device components. Transistors are found in electronic circuits, and are used to control how the electricity flows within the circuit.

Transmission: To deliver a large quantity of something like electricity over a long distance, so it can be distributed to customers at its destination. Electricity is generated in a big generation plant, then delivered to your city by a transmission system.

Ultraviolet: A nearly blue light is part of our surroundings, that we cannot see. It is the part of sunlight that can give us a sunburn even when it is cloudy. It is also good for destroying harmful bacteria.

About the Author

James is a management consultant and a mechanical engineer. He works in heavy industries, and often in out-of-the-way locations, helping them improve the performance of their physical plant and equipment. He has worked in the navy, petrochemicals, oil refining, ship-building, aircraft maintenance, avionics, and as a consultant in resource industries, pulp and paper, facilities management, health care, logistics, mining, mineral processing and refining, electric and gas utilities, packaging, food, automotive, water and waste water utilities.